You are Love

THE DISCOVERY OF HAPPINESS

SARA SPOWART, PhD, LMFT, MPA, DMFT(c), RYT, CCHT

THE DISCOVERY OF HAPPINESS

Dedicated to everyone everywhere.

You are me and I am You, I see You in Me and I see myself in You…How can there be separation there?? Only the center I is there.

—Gajraj Delbehera

TABLE OF CONTENTS

FOREWORD

Overview of My Story

This book is about experiences, discoveries, and insights that have come to me during this life. My hope is that sharing these can be helpful to others and support them in their life journeys and challenges. Pain and struggle have been my biggest teachers, as well as love. Love in all its variations and the spectrum across which it exists are incredibly powerful forces. There is nothing quite like experiencing love in friendships, families, and relationships, as well as the pain from these relationships. However, instead of pushing against pain, you can accept it and send love to it. Some of the best things and greatest positive transformations only come about because of pain.

The insights in this book have also come from many illnesses and multiple near-death experiences I've had as well as many terrible things I've seen and experienced. The highs and lows of life have been blessings in disguise that pushed my perspective beyond the usual way of seeing the world and towards a greater, more expansive understanding of reality. This isn't a perspective I share with anyone except the very closest people in my life whom I feel understand and have some similar insights and understandings. I suppose the main reason for this is it didn't feel appropriate or feel like it made sense to discuss the things I talk about in the book until now. However, I feel this perspective is ongoing, ever-deepening, and evolving, and might be of some help to others to make others' lives better. So, it is now time to share.

Overview and Goal of This Book

The aim of this book is to help assist you in beginning or growing your understanding of your true nature and interconnectedness with everything and everyone around you. My hope is that after reading this book you will have a deeper understanding of the way we are all one. There is a universal energy that flows and makes up absolutely everything, and also manifests into infinite forms. That energy that is in you, is also in me. We are all connected. Understanding this brings about a deeper level of joy, empathy, harmony, happiness, peace and love in our lives. This positive shift flows over and positively impacts everything we do.

CHAPTER 1
SHIFTING YOUR PERSPECTIVE

*"The difference of enlightenment is just
one perspective shift."*

Shift Your Perspective: By Being Thankful

I'm thankful for everything, including the so-called good and bad, because it has all served a purpose. When we allow it or can detach enough, everything can be used for our growth and expansion. The more you expand and grow, the better you feel and the better life can be. Growth can be painful but, in the long term, we always feel best when we grow, learn, and expand. Life becomes lighter, more loving, kinder, and more peaceful, and you begin to see yourself in everyone and everything.

Some of the major events of my life that pushed me towards understanding and change were difficult family struggles, family addiction, challenges with eating disorders, various experiences I've had with sexual harassment, very abusive relationships, and even two men trying to take me at one point when I worked in East Africa twenty years ago. Furthermore, I've had multiple life-threatening asthma attacks where I almost died, and had severe life-threatening allergic reactions where I had to be hospitalized because I was unable to breathe. In addition to this, I was very ill with typhoid fever when I worked in Tanzania. I came close to dying from this because I was incorrectly diagnosed and treated; the illness lasted three to four weeks. I had malaria when I worked in Ghana. I've had to be treated for tuberculosis I probably got in Russia and also survived dengue fever in Costa Rica. I've also now had COVID-19 numerous times and one of them was definitely a life-threatening experience. The many years of work I've done as a mental health therapist and social worker in the United States and abroad with victims and survivors of violence, poverty, horrific trauma, human trafficking, torture, and rape have also left an impression on me about suffering and the different types of suffering that individuals experience. When I worked with survivors of violence, I was followed, stalked, and harassed by traffickers and perpetrators of violence who were hurting my clients.

The pain I saw and experienced collectively from these situations led me to think the world is not about making us happy or following a formula for success. There's something much deeper going on. I was recently reminded of the television show *The Good Place*, in which all of the characters have passed away and they are in a fake heaven. I realized that a lot of the pain of that situation came from them not understanding the nature of their reality clearly. When they realized they were in a type of hell (the fake heaven), suddenly all of the challenges they experienced were a lot more manageable and less upsetting. In a similar fashion, when we can look around and understand that suffering is a natural part of life and it *is* the reality of this world, it is less of a shock every time challenges happen. Like the show *The Good Place*, the characters realized that suffering was a normal part of their reality because they were in a fake heaven.

I also learned this when I worked in rape crisis counseling in Pinellas County, Florida, and with survivors of violence and trafficking for many years. Many of the people I worked with struggled greatly with what we saw on a daily basis and there was a high turnover rate. Something I realized at one point was to stop reacting to every incident of abuse, rape, and violence that a client reported. I and others I worked with would feel upset by the things we heard and saw because we felt the world should not be this way. We felt that every abuse was wrong and the world was supposed to be better; we felt abuse was abnormal. It was like encountering something every day, all day, that you felt shouldn't be happening. When I realized the tragic reality that there is a certain normalcy to violence and abuse, and it is highly prevalent in many forms everywhere, this shifted everything for me. Instead of feeling upset every time by different situations I felt shouldn't be happening, I realized, *no, this is the reality of the world we live in.* It is a world full of many types of abuse, oftentimes from the people closest to you.

According to some Buddhist traditions, this is the realm or world of 10,000 sorrows and 10,000 joys. This means that, like the TV show *The Good Place*, no matter what we do, there is always going to be something painful that happens. It's just part of the reality of this world. We can work to decrease suffering and pain but there will always be some degree of it no matter how small because of the illusion of the reality of this world. The more we buy into following a formula for success or happiness, or follow society's rules and look outside ourselves for measurements of well-being and success, the more disconnected we become from the truth of who we are.

The amount of suffering, trauma, and pain I've experienced over this lifetime has collectively been the perfect amount to trigger the breakthroughs and insights that have come through me. In a way, I suppose every insight seems to have some kind of cost. Nothing comes for free.☺ When I learned to reframe pain and suffering as my friend, here to teach me something so I could grow to be a better version of myself and not feel like a victim, everything changed.

However, inviting and welcoming in your growth and expansion is not for the faint of heart. You have to be a bit brave. Just the last few weeks alone, I've been meditating, praying, and wishing to grow to a higher, next-level self. I've been getting my wish, but as always, we should be careful what we wish for. In the last month alone (while writing this), I had another near-death experience where I almost suffocated to death from an asthma attack and had to use multiple pens. I easily could have died—again. I also had a major robbery in my home when I was gone. Someone high on cocaine broke down the door and $30,000 of my things were stolen and many of them were irreplaceable family heirlooms. In addition to that, I've had very difficult client situations in which children were being abused. I had to deal with lawyers and the court systems to protect children against abusers in a system that does not sufficiently believe or listen to children. My fiancée also had a near-death experience during this time. He almost drowned surfing. Someone else who was surfing near him also almost drowned because they were pulled by the current towards some cliffs and couldn't get out. Yes, these are just the things from the last month. Again, I have to remember my wish to grow and expand to become my next-level self so I can serve the world at a higher level.

I have to say, for all the challenges, they continue to function as a mechanism to bring about deeper insights, expansion, and growth. Somehow, and don't ask me how I feel these recent events freed me of other layers I didn't even know I had. It was like some kind of clearing and a deeper letting go; and the more that happens, the more I learn to let go. Control is not the answer. You can do the best you can to protect yourself from harm of course, but there are many limits to this. So much is out of our control, and sometimes it's best to let go, surrender, and trust the flow. When we get 'ourselves' out of the way, we become free to go with this flow and become higher versions of ourselves. Our freedom comes from getting over ourselves, being free of ourselves, and connecting to what is bigger and greater. It does not come from everything going right and going just the way we want. In fact, many times it seems that everything going just the way we want doesn't really help us grow at all. Our greatest expansion can come from getting what we *don't want*, or some random, left-field things there's no way we could have predicted. Thankfulness and insight regarding our challenges can mean these things happen for our growth, development, and expansion; somehow, they can ultimately be turned into positive, enlightening, powerful things.

Shift Your Perspective: Through A Deeper Knowing

There is a greater knowledge and understanding of reality beyond just normal human understanding. It is a knowing that is sublime, peaceful, content, and even joyful, beyond reason and logic—an inherent joy that can exist in every one of us. By focusing on the wellness of our emotional and internal states, we naturally shift and impact our outer realities. Seeing it—really seeing the absolute importance of getting the inside right—is different from just hearing that your internal state is connected to your external state. They are not separate. In fact, one informs and helps create the other.

This doesn't mean abandoning your journey towards accomplishing certain goals in the external reality, or not taking care of life essentials like paying for food, clothing, housing, and so on. However, the 'external' does not need to dictate the state of the internal. The internal state is of primary importance and has a direct impact on the external. Your external circumstances will become better when the internal is improved. Also, ironically, it may not seem to happen as quickly as you'd like, but when the internal state is healed, external circumstances tend to appear better, even if not immediately. Another way of putting this is that when you feel and experience a state of wholeness internally, everything in your outside reality begins to shift as well. Once you begin to feel whole, your life only improves to a greater and greater extent.

Reflection Question

Taking a moment now, maybe you can ask yourself,
How am I feeling? What do I notice?

Shift Your Perspective: By Investing in Your Internal State

Understanding this shift can take some faith and be challenging. However, if you start to understand that investing in your internal state is one of the most important things for the external reality, it becomes easier to do. Investing in your internal state can take many forms. Some of these forms include improving your diet, exercise, and sleep routine so that your internal well-being is improved. Sometimes this may mean investing in regular therapy for yourself or making tiny, baby-step changes in your life to improve your mindset.

Even if you take small steps one by one, making the shifts you are able to make is important for greater overall changes in your life circumstances. By taking care of our present moment reality, we are investing not only in our future but also in our external circumstances. Yes, it's true that there is some value to denial and repression at times. If situations become too overwhelming or difficult, we may not be ready to confront or deal with them. However, by addressing as much as we can in our inner state of being, we will create much more joy, peace, and happiness in our lives. This is because at our core, we are energetic beings.

If you don't know what I mean here, just think about how you feel when someone really negative and unhappy walks into a small room.

Can you feel it? Do you notice?

Most of us do.

Shift Your Perspective: By Clearing Away the Old

We are physical beings, but at a larger level, we are actually energetic beings. All of our experiences and everything we encounter are in many ways a manifestation of energy. If we neglect our energetic state, either intentionally or from ignorance or lack of awareness, we hurt ourselves and unconsciously bring things into our lives that are not healthy for us. The greater the level of layers and attachments you have, the more that must fall away and blow up in your life in order for you to shift and see more clearly. The falling away of everything that is untrue and the openness to let go is one of the most liberating things that can happen to you.

One of the things I see with clients, and I guess in general that is most painful, is the attachment people have to their identities and what they *think* makes them who they are. You may hold onto your title as a husband, wife, mother, father, grandparent, boss, CEO, artist, teacher, athlete, or sick person. It doesn't really matter. Identity attachment is attachment and will cause a lot of pain. The reality is that anything you have to fight for or reassert repeatedly in order for it to be true is not actually true. Something that is naturally true just is. You don't need to fight for it and you aren't threatened by something that counteracts it. You feel safe and comfortable in it. It just is; you don't have to construct it over and over and you can't lose it.

What is underneath the surface of all the layers is just the energy of you, the observer, a consciousness that is greater than just the individual you. You are much more connected to everything than you realize, but it's necessary to peel away and clear the attachments and layers to get there and see it clearly. This inner essence was always there and will always be there, but you were distracted by the outer layers of reality and what appeared on the outside to be real, true, and important. Distraction by the drama of life takes away from the awareness of the consciousness and core that is observing it (i.e., you).

Practice

Can you sit for a few minutes right now with your eyes closed? Sit, trying to place your consciousness to look back at yourself. Who is there? Who is doing the observing here and what is being observed?

Shift Your Perspective: Through Authentic Living

By becoming fully, authentically you, your perspective will shift quickly in a more positive way. You will also become more aware of the invisible flow and life stream more quickly. Living authentically helps you to become more filled with joy, peace, energy, and contentment. You want to be present in your life and enjoy it. There is less resistance and unhappiness when we are being fully, authentically ourselves in how we live our lives, and we feel much more connected. To do this, many times we have to learn how to get out of our own way. The more individuated and truly, fully authentic you are, the happier you are. The more you feel suppressed, controlled, and forced to live a life that feels unnatural to you, the worse you will feel. You will look for things to cover up and manage the pain. In a way, it doesn't matter how much you try to cover up the pain of not being fully, truly who you are. Eventually, no coping mechanism will ultimately work and you may find the best solution is to face yourself and confront the things that hurt you.

Some mechanisms to deal with managing pain and avoid the process of becoming authentically ourselves include things like living on automatic pilot, being checked out and being somewhat mentally disassociated. A classic example is driving a car and arriving at your destination without paying attention or remembering how you got there. Other forms of not living authentically can include things like 1) avoidance instead of acceptance, 2) thinking about ideas instead of directly experiencing, 3) judging or fixing instead of observing, 4) reacting instead of responding, and 5) practicing unhealthy habits instead of appropriate self-care.

Other ways of avoiding our true selves or living authentically can be the stories we tell ourselves or the inauthentic identities we portray to cope with and manage emotions. For example, someone who is a violent abuser may tell himself or herself that he or she is the victim and whatever hurt the person causes to others is justified. Self-centered focus and low levels of empathy can keep us living reactively, in accordance with whatever we perceive feels pleasant and not what feels unpleasant. Through mindfulness, self-compassion, and paying attention to when we feel most naturally ourselves, we can begin to create lives that feel more in flow, lighter, and happier.

The alternative to this is to live in denial or ignore the way things really are and continue with painful reactive patterns indefinitely. Two of the greatest obstacles I see with clients are 1) their belief that what they are experiencing is unique to them and their fault, and 2) ongoing negative reactivity and emotional responses to the way things are. What they can't see is the patterns I see in many clients going through similar things because of the nature of reality that we live in. People may feel their experiences of loneliness, isolation, or poor relationships are unique to them, but these are prevalent issues and recurring patterns I see often in sessions. Across the board, we are absolutely more similar than different. Often what we experience to be unique to us or seems to be our fault is actually something experienced by the masses and a collective issue. Like abuse survivors, we oftentimes blame ourselves or others for our pain and unhappiness instead of considering the possibility that it is just the way things are.

Non-acceptance or self-blame causes reactions to the pain repeatedly and does not heal it.

My personal experiences with extreme illness as well as my work with many clients have left important impressions on me and my feelings of purpose. Because of them, for better and worse, I can't go back to seeing things in the same way anymore. I am broken from seeing my path as directed by particular goals and structures created by society, family, and culture. If you have enough experiences and question the nature of reality often enough, you break free from the cycles and patterns and can step back with detached clarity and purpose.

There are programs from religious organizations, schools, governments, media, families, cultures, societies, and workplaces. You name it and there is some kind of idea on how to do it "correctly." These programs also focus less on internal experience and more on external behavior. A good question to consider might be: *what programs currently exist in my life?*

Reflection Questions:

What program have you been following?

What does meeting basic needs have to do with how you are doing on the inside?

What if our greatest expansion is largely about a shift in perspective?

Shift Your Perspective: Through Commitment

I once heard an old story from Buddhism that if you want to understand the nature of reality clearly, you must want it as much as you want to breathe if you were forced underwater. You must be 1000% committed to this understanding and journey, and never stop or assume you have achieved it. You should realize that as every layer unfolds and drops away, there is no "having" and there is in fact no "it." These are mental constructs that make greater sense with every unfolding of understanding. You must decide to be open to whatever needs to happen in order to learn and shift into whomever you need to shift into becoming, or rather unbecoming. Learn to listen to your intuition and the small things that bring you joy, following them like a lit-up pathway, and surrendering to every direction they take you.

Know that there are layers upon layers of self that will fall away, and never assume you have reached the end. With every falling away, you get closer to the limitlessness and endlessness that is infinite. As levels of deeper love appear and reveal themselves in everything around us, it becomes clear that love makes up the nature of reality and the energy of everything around us and in us. In this energy of love, everything is connected and is part of everything and anything.

The information in this book is important because right now we seem to be in a period of rapid change and growth in the world. The seemingly solid structures and beliefs we have held may not appear as solid as they once were. There can be a much greater sense of uncertainty now. The feeling of dependability in life that if you do certain things then you will have a certain reliable outcome does not generally match up as well now. Life is arguably chaotic and complicated and I don't see this changing anytime soon. In fact, things continue to speed up, not slow down. With this increasingly complex, changing reality, the old appearance of structure and stability is falling away. Increasingly we need to be adaptable, resilient, and able to handle unpredictable change and life circumstances. Being open, continuing to learn, and remaining somewhat unattached to outcomes and circumstances are critical survival skills for thriving in today's world, despite any and all appearances of instability and change.

The old ways of being protected seem to be changing and falling away. The solutions of the past—making sure you have the "right" education, are married at the "right" time or to a certain type of person, or make sure you follow a particular path in life—provide less stability and protection from suffering than before. Our realities are changing and adapting. They do not keep the same momentum and patterns that they used to. Therefore, it is critical in the future to learn new ways of thriving in this world and to adapt to new understandings of ourselves and our lived experiences.

Essentially what I'm saying is that in order to thrive in our world now and in the future, we are being pushed to evolve and grow into someone maybe we've never been before.

CHAPTER 2

PAIN

Pain: Your Relationship to Pain

Before and at the beginning of my Ph.D. almost ten years ago, I naively thought that all answers could be found through learning and academics. This wasn't always the case because at other times I thought the answers could be found in travel, relationships, family, religion, dieting, or attaining the perfect weight. I went through a lot of exploration thinking one thing after another held mysterious answers that I didn't even realize I was seeking. The incessant craving and searching for more started from as young as I can remember, and was always part of what drove me.

When I reflect on it here, I suppose I started seeking and looking for answers when I was five years old and started to look around and question my reality. I think I was trying to make sense of the pain I saw around me in my family and in society. It sounds a bit extreme at age five or six to do this, but that was me. I started out seeking from a young age. I didn't even know what I was looking for. However, I was determined to learn what would make my parents, my grandparents, my brothers, the kids I knew, and the children I learned about who were hungry and in poverty in other countries through Church sponsorship, happy and at peace. I tried to find answers to this. I wanted to help. I remember being seven years old, getting a notebook and clipboard, and asking my middle brother questions about his feelings, trying to help him feel better. I had absolutely no training to be playing therapist to my five-year-old brother at the time. Somehow, I felt that exploring his pain would lead to answers on how to solve it. I also wore a necklace I found that said "May all beings be happy and free." This is just how my mind operated and how I viewed the world. I felt there wasn't supposed to be the suffering and pain I saw, both the invisible emotional pain and the external suffering.

I guess you could say I was sensitive and other people's pain both hurt and worried me. For whatever reason, I tasked myself or felt it was my mission to find the "answer" so that everyone could be happy. You could call it a five- or seven-year-old with codependency on steroids, but really it was more than that. I had extreme empathy and could feel the things others didn't say out loud or verbalize. I could sense an emotional or energetic reality most seemed to ignore or miss. As the years went on, I tried all kinds of things. I wrote affirmations for my mom. I tried to get perfect grades for my dad. I tried to comfort and help my brothers as best as I could. I tried to be the perfect weight for my grandma. I left my grandpa alone. As an adolescent, I led a campaign of fasting to raise more than $10,000 for starving children in impoverished countries.

I learned to navigate what seemed to help give temporary relief to the pain I saw and felt around me in the world.

It wasn't anyone's fault; it is the pain of being human and basically being confused. However, my reason for sharing this, is that this search began once I started to have some understanding of pain around me. I am happy to report that since 2011 or 2012, I've begun to have some major breakthroughs, insights, and success in understanding what the hell is going on here literally. These insights came on their own through a lot of pain, meditation, and desperation. I feel that anything that has come through me has been a gift. I have been blessed and need to pass it on as best I can to however many people as possible. As a family friend of ours used to say, "Life isn't supposed to feel like this. It isn't supposed to be this way."

What he meant is we aren't supposed to be suffering and as confused as so many of us generally are.

Part of the thing here is that the pain is part of the path. The suffering and the struggle actually point the way and can call in the insights and understanding we so desperately want. What I realized on this ever-unfolding journey that still continues is that when pain arises, most of humanity gets stuck in it. It's like the hurt and confusion are so great it becomes stuck in us and we become trapped. We often don't learn from our families or from society how to manage when we get stuck. In fact, we learn the opposite: we learn we are the victims of things that happen. Another way of saying it is that life is happening to us and we are the innocent bystanders of whatever happens or may happen. The reality is that there can be a lot of horrible things that happen in our lives. This is absolutely true. However, sometimes trying to understand the "why" behind these things can get us stuck and trapped in the loop. We want to get out of the loop of pain and painful thoughts, not keep entertaining ourselves within the loop and getting deeper and deeper.

Mental Exercise: Holographic Universe

I would like you to close your eyes and imagine for a moment that we live in a holographic world or a holographic universe. This does not mean it's not real; in fact, this *is* reality. It's as real as it gets. However, because it's holographic, it is changeable and always shifting. Things come into our reality randomly that sometimes match up to our plans and ideas of how things should and do go. At other times, things happen from leftfield and absolutely do not align with our ideas.

Now imagine in this holographic universe and world, every time something happens that feels good or you like, you accept it as normal reality. By contrast, everything that is unpleasant sparks pain, or sparks questions, this holographic universe wants you to understand better. The pain is meant to snap you out of the holographic attachment and question what is going on.

Knowing it wants you to understand it much better, what do you think it will do? (I forgot to mention in this scenario that the holographic universe has its own intelligence.) If you go along with everything and don't question much when things are going well, but stop everything and obsess when you are suffering, what does it hear? It hears, "Okay, so when there is pain and suffering, they question things more and they want to understand everything more? My greatest wish is that they fully connect with me and understand everything that is going on. However, they will have to keep suffering until we have some breakthroughs and they let go of their old ways of thinking."

This is a basic way of explaining the situation, but it's also a helpful example for understanding what the hell is going on here, literally.

As another spiritual teacher I love once said, "Have you ever noticed none of this really makes sense?" It seems like it makes sense, but the more you experience and the more you see, it doesn't make sense at all. In many ways, life is random, chaotic, and uncontrollable. It has a mind of its own. Therefore, we are called to dive deeper. We are called to go further into ourselves and into an openness to understand. We are called to look up from the daily grind of the perception of our lives and become open to whatever larger forces are trying to show us.

We have so much to learn and see.

Will you be open to listening and humble enough to learn?

If not, I must warn you, these universal powers that seek to evolve and enhance you will continue with the suffering until you become open and humble enough to learn and listen. Some people only need the whisper of a suggestion to question things and make changes. Other people need to be hit with a metaphoric baseball bat. This force that wants us to grow, evolve, get out of our own way, and be freed from unhealthy cycles, is stronger than any of us and has its own intelligent agenda.

Why not skip a ton of pain and suffering and decide at this moment, right now, to be humble and open, to listen, to learn, be connected, and try new ways of thinking if necessary? The decision is yours. You can be stubborn, hold out, and cling to your normal or old way of seeing the world. However, this larger force or power is greater than you and will ultimately always win. It is an awesome force and will turn your life upside down repeatedly to get you to crack like a nut if that's what it takes. It's badass energy and stays consistently badass no matter what you may try to do to dictate the terms of your life. If there are larger things for you to learn, it won't stop shaking up your life until you learn and embrace them.

To reflect, what are some cycles you are currently caught in?

How do you get in your own way or continue to live inauthentically?

Pain: Detaching from Pain

I won't go into the details of my life experiences mostly because I have learned that the details of the story aren't in fact critical to understanding the concepts and insights. I've also found that the more you let go of the story (and really any story) and are grateful for the insights you have, the more insights and understanding that come. The more frustrated and obsessive you are about *why* things aren't going the way you want, the deeper you can become trapped in the loop. Someone can be living in a multi-million-dollar home or in poverty and both be suffering. Suffering is suffering. It doesn't matter where you're living, how educated you are, or what your background or income is—there is always pain and suffering because of the nature of reality. To be human is to experience pain at different times. This pain can be extreme or mild, but the pain is pain. There are variations in the pain, of course. Pain takes on different forms, and we need compassion for ourselves and others to address it. However, there is a way to understand the pain. Deeper levels of realization create less pain. Essentially, the deeper reason for our pain is that we don't understand the nature of reality clearly.

So often we can feel that life is unfair and everything is happening *to us*—that we are victims of our circumstances and our lives. Feeling we are victims may mean we feel there are a lot of stressful or awful things happening to us. This is one level of reality and understanding, and I will talk about this further in the book. I refer to this as the victim stage, or you could say the victim perspective. However, there are many layers to understanding reality and each is better than the last. It's like a kaleidoscope that you turn to see something new. There are multiple lenses and multiple vantage points from which to view the world. Another helpful example might be if you've ever had prescription glasses to which you could add different color lenses. You can have yellow lenses, red ones, ones for glare, sunglass lenses, and so on. These lenses stick to the original frame through magnetization. When you look out of each lens, the world looks different and you see different perspectives.

Although the kaleidoscope and the different color lenses are somewhat simplistic examples, the same concept is true with deeper levels of realization. Realization means understanding reality, its meaning, and the unfolding process of seeing reality more clearly.

A deeper realization may be just one shift in perspective away from where you are now.

Reflection Question: How can you shift your perspective?

Our individual histories or backgrounds (both known and unknown) contribute to our mental loops or 'programs.' This collective background of life experiences can skew or slant your perspective of the world, or the lens through which you see life. Therefore, the first step is questioning and investigating your initial perspective of the world. Sometimes our idea of how reality works is not totally correct. For example, someone may think that "all people are out for themselves" or "you can't trust anyone." These all-or-nothing, absolute statements can help to identify red flags of skewed perspectives or lenses on the world. It can be hard to see your blind spots or areas where you are slanted and misperceiving reality. However, these all-or-nothing, absolute statements are good places to start. They can help you investigate the negative beliefs you have. Unfortunately, and for whatever reason, many of our skewed ideas are probably more negative rather than positive. Therefore, looking at the negative is another good place to start with addressing this.

Another way of considering this is to think of our perspective of the world as a dirty car windshield or window. If you don't clean the windshield or window, dirt and other things build up and change the view when you are looking out from the window. You can't see as clearly. Now imagine that your life is this way. Your vision or lens is not as clear as you might think it is. It may seem that you are completely reasonable and logical, but maybe there is a bit of a skew that you aren't even fully aware of. Questioning our perceptions is the first step. This is not to say your perspective is wrong, but questioning helps you to detach from it a bit so you can see more clearly.

Bringing self-kindness, self-compassion, and gentleness to yourself can all help with fostering clearer insight and understanding while staying somewhat detached. However, everything discussed in this book is being pointed to. The essence of *Realizing Love* is having the clearest perspective possible, going beyond holding onto any one thing or situation, and beyond unrelenting attachment and clinging. Rumi supposedly said, "Out beyond ideas of wrongdoing and right doing there is a field. I'll meet you there." This does not necessarily mean there is no right or wrong and you should have no opinions of things. Rather, it points to the concept that how we label our reality, the judgments, and solidified descriptions we give to just about anything, get in the way of our happiness, and taint or color our perspectives.

Aside from this, when we are very attached to certain perspectives, we are likely to create a sense of separation and judgment between ourselves and everything outside of us. When we parcel out and judge everything around us, we also create a separation between ourselves and our reality. We create the further illusion of separation between ourselves and others. It may sound strange, but that in itself is a kind of violence. Violence is not always overt and physical; it can occur first in the mind through judgment, separation, and divisions we create between ourselves and others, and even the divisions we create within ourselves.

Getting to a place of internal wholeness or completeness, and stopping separation and division, creates peace and joy within ourselves. Again, the words to describe this are just words pointing to a lived experience and concept. The lived experience of wholeness is most helpful.

CHAPTER 3

THE BEAUTY OF A HUMAN LIFE

The Beauty of a Human Life: Uniqueness

Living a human life can be very meaningful and precious. This is because we always have a mix of positive and negative emotions, pleasure and pain. This mix of pleasure and pain can push and challenge us to seek out and open our minds to greater insights. The irony is that if we have too much pleasure and life is too easy and positive, there is absolutely no incentive to learn, grow, and push ourselves. In a way, you can become numb and complacent because of the ease of everything. On the other hand, if everything is too difficult, there are too many challenges and too much pain, and you feel trapped in your life, you are also not able to move forward and grow, learn, and investigate like you might otherwise. Therefore, this mixture of positive and negative is hopefully enough of a blended contrast to push you to grow and learn and maybe desire to become a more evolved version of yourself. The more 'evolved' you are, the less you suffer and the happier you will feel. With that being said, some people do seem to require more pain and difficulty than others to be pushed to grow. One of the greatest gifts you can give yourself is learning from other people's pain, mistakes, and lessons so you don't have to repeat them yourself. If you can learn by observation of others around you and not needlessly copy harmful lessons, it's like fast-tracking your evolution.

The Beauty of a Human Life: Human Pain

We will all experience a certain amount of suffering and stress in our lives. It seems inevitable. In reality, just the daily functioning of being human requires some level of mental, emotional, and physical stress, even when we have all our needs met and are generally happy. Stress and pain from stress are also partly self-inflicted. With some people, you could say it's largely self-inflicted. For example, for one person, getting the wrong order on a breakfast item in a café is literally enough for that person to feel his or her entire morning or day is ruined. However, for another person, even extremely life-changing events, such as losing a job or a marriage, may not upset them that much. The person may even feel relieved or have less stress. Therefore, the respective pain created due to something occurring in one's life is not necessarily due to the thing itself. The suffering is often in relation to one's perception and his or her view of the world.

Another perspective on this could be to imagine we live in a universe that is intelligent by design. It loves us so much that it really wants us to see reality more deeply, and get out of repeating, harmful cycles we may be trapped in. Specifically, this larger force wants to free us of the mental, emotional, or physical loops we may be unable to get out of. Sometimes to do that, it's necessary to become extremely uncomfortable in those cycles and situations until we feel we can't stand them anymore and must make a change. This can also be what is meant by hitting rock bottom when we decide we can't continue living a certain way anymore. If there is a point or goal, you could say the aim of the pain is to push ourselves out of our own way and out of the cycles we are stuck in. By doing this, we can maybe get to a space beyond points and end goals. This is a space of limitless, infinite love that has no boundaries or conditions. The ego is no longer a barrier and we are literally in a state of joy.

"Close your eyes, fall in love, stay there" —Rumi

The above quote from Rumi points to this state of joy. It is probably not really about falling in love in the romantic sense. What is most important is to "close your eyes" meaning *getting yourself, your labels, judgments, attachments, and the things you cling to for reality* out of the way. Stop the attachment to the world you see and you will experience an infinite limitless field of love that is pure positive potential beyond our mental concepts. "Stay there" means to exist in that space where your attachment to labels, mental constructs, and things is gone and you are existing as love—existing as spaciousness and being. These are amazingly simple, straightforward, and clear instructions on "being joy," "being yourself," and being pure consciousness. Being human is a unique and precious experience in contrast to any other creature on Earth. We have the ability to self-reflect, create change and understand our consciousness and reality in ways that other beings on this planet simply cannot.

The things we take most for granted and are the most normal to us are often the problems that keep us trapped in cycles. This is why pain can be so valuable; it shakes things up—a lot. It has the potential to make us stop and question our lives and our perspectives and to question and investigate normalcy and reality. What do you do when you hit rock bottom? You start to stop, detach, and question things. You reflect on yourself and your life. Otherwise, why would you do it? Meditation is another incredible and excellent way to begin to transcend these limitations and to investigate and question what is normal. However, people don't usually begin meditation unless they are uncomfortable and trying to learn how to manage difficult situations, or are in crisis. Unless it's a cultural norm or a person is being somehow forced to meditate, someone usually begins to change because he or she is suffering and struggling with something. We look inward when the outside becomes too painful and/or we just can't make sense of it anymore and are hoping to find a new way to obtain some answers.

Human beings are fortunate in some ways because, even though we often make ourselves feel or act in crazy ways because of what is happening in our minds, we also have the ability to have insight into why and how our experiences are happening. Unlike other creatures, we can question everything and anything. We can search for a higher meaning and understanding to get beyond the current state of mind. If there was only constant happiness, contentment, and pleasure, there would be very little in-depth reflection. We would be living in a state of mostly relaxed, heavenly bliss. Although that's wonderful, it doesn't allow for much introspection or detachment and allows us to search for what is beyond the appearance and surface understanding of things.

When everything is wonderful, we can become complacent, checked out, and almost too relaxed. Have you ever noticed that it's only when something is really painful or there is a lot of suffering that you get help? If, for example, you have many relationships end, you may only then start questioning what relationships mean to you, what happens in them, and what you think and feel concerning relationships. It's nearly always the pain, not the pleasure, that leads to questioning and deeper introspection. This is unfortunate but seems to be the nature of reality at this point. Within suffering, there are tremendous amounts of insight, understanding, questioning, and breakthroughs beyond ourselves that can take place. This is not possible for other creatures such as dogs, cats, or cows for example. They are sentient beings and should be treated with kindness and love as important creatures. However, they do not have the capacity to reflect on themselves and question reality as humans do.

The things that happen in our lives and everyday realities are opportunities for noticing and observing reality. They are opportunities that no other creature (that I'm aware of at this point) has. We live in a world that is a blend of pain and joy. It is a never-ending blend of the two. When you think that everything is great and will continue to be that way, it all falls apart. On the other hand, when you think that life will never change and everything is awful, it changes again. You may experience this mix of joy and pain in a day, an hour, or five minutes. We push away or resist the pain because we don't like it. We hold on to what feels good or even cling to it, and we feel neutral towards things that don't seem to bring us pleasure or pain. Many of us live our lives in this way. We tend to follow whatever we think will bring the greatest amount of pleasure and the least amount of pain, and not notice the 'neutral' things. This can lead to living in fear of things that could hurt us, clinging to things that bring pleasure, or fearing losing what we thought made us happy. It can also mean we miss a lot of life that is in the perceived 'neutral' things by disregarding them and not giving them value. By ignoring much of what is neutral, we disregard the majority of reality and probably obsess over what seems to bring us the greatest joy or pain.

It's like zeroing in on certain things while ignoring others. It means putting a lens on reality so you aren't actually seeing it clearly, and probably missing much more than you know.

The Beauty of a Human Life: Being an Observer

There are ways to rise above being trapped in a seemingly endless loop of gravitating toward pleasure and resisting or fighting against the pain. One of the solutions is to become more of an observer in your life. This does not mean that you are cold and uncaring. Rather, it means that you are learning to notice. Instead of the normal operating mechanism being reacting or even responding, it becomes just noticing. Noticing in itself is very powerful and can reduce the intensity and frequency of emotions. By noticing, we become more aware and detached. Instead of reacting to whatever is happening or may appear to be happening around you, just notice it. A major principle of mindfulness and mindful living is the practice of noticing. You take note of everything you experience within you emotionally, mentally, and physically, and what is happening or occurring outside of your world.

With mindfulness comes the understanding that when you are in or living something, it's hard to see the whole of it. If you are too close to something, it's hard to see it because you're lacking contrast and objectivity. However, when you detach and can be more of a third-party objectively viewing it, it's much easier to see and have insights than if you were in it. Another way of putting this to use is the metaphor of trying to explain water to a fish. The fish has lived in water its entire life; it was born in water and will likely die in the water. Therefore, it's practically impossible for it to understand life outside of the water. If the fish had the cognitive capacity and ability to live for some moments outside the water and see the contrasting experiences of reality, then the insights about its lived reality and what water and air are would be huge. Of course, a fish can't survive outside of the water or reflect on the difference between living in water or the air. This is merely an analogy for detaching yourself from what you've always known and experienced in order to have a better, larger view of what is really happening.

Similarly, I've found that by taking more of a bird's eye view whenever possible, I'm able to discern a lot more insights and understanding about reality than when I'm in the thick of the drama. When you're in drama, it's easy to get sucked into whatever the newest incident, pain, excitement, strong emotion, frustration, or difficulty is.

The Beauty of a Human Life: Levels of Realization

In this book, everything comes from directly lived experiences and the insights and understandings that developed as a result. None of what I write about here comes directly from studying. However, studying has been part of my journey. Experiences with studying have impacted my ability to have these insights and probably some of the wording on how I express the concepts.

I find I'm still in awe when there is a new insight and I have to remind myself that this is an ever-unfolding process that just keeps getting better. The nature of reality is the ultimate, and the ultimate is limitless. There is no "getting there." Reality is more of a realization that you don't get "there" and the destination is not an end. The destination is limitless, infinite expansiveness. It is an ever-greater unfolding of higher energy shifts and deeper levels of understanding. I would like to cut to the "end" here for the sake of everyone reading this. The "end," if you want to call it that, is the experience of a total connection and oneness and unity with all that exists in a space of infinite limitlessness. It's seeing beyond just the outer appearance of reality to a deeper level of energetic connection and unity. It's kind of like being able to see the light or energy in everything, everywhere around you.

There is a field of energy that permeates and makes up absolutely everything. When you can see you are part of this and everything is this light or energy in manifested form, there is an all-encompassing unity and interconnectedness. You get yourself out of the way finally and you see that *you are the other*, you are the tree, the grass, the sky, the other person—everything. The same energy that is in everything else is in you and the other. There is no real separation, only the view or perspective of separation. The separation is an illusion of our projection and what we're able to see with our eyes and physical senses.

This all-pervasive energy or light may seem or feel like different things to different people. It could seem like a sense of peacefulness, a sense of love, joy, compassion, contentment, or understanding, or a feeling of relief like everything makes sense finally. Whatever arises, don't feel like you need to cling to it. It's like holding onto the air; you can't do it. Through a relaxed detachment, through allowing and letting go, you may begin to see these deeper layers. It's not through obsessing, clinging, or forcing that you connect to the deeper layers. Rather, it is by opening up and letting go in this state of being—a sort of nameless state of being that cannot really be explained sufficiently with words or concepts. It is a lived experience of spaciousness, unity, connection, and love. Like watching a butterfly float from flower to flower, you just let it be; it's best not to try to trap it. Its beauty comes from the seemingly effortless color, grace, and flow of its being. Eventually, over time, this perspective becomes more integrated into your reality. Not only do you experience the outer projection of the world like everyone else, but you also live in this incredible understanding that everything is energy, made of the energy of love, limitless, and one field in manifested form.

The Beauty of a Human Life:
The Struggle of Shifting Perspective

Ultimately, and even in the medium term, life is much better when we notice our cycles and work to disintegrate them, letting go of the attachment to self and the story of self. The lives of everyone around us are also much better. However, it doesn't mean it's a naturally smooth process at all times. Some common pitfalls with this process are having insights and major shifts either momentarily or for a period of time, becoming attached to them, and thinking you are special or somehow superior because you are able to see reality more clearly than others. It may seem bizarre and almost counterintuitive for someone to think he or she is somehow superior after having insights of everything being one manifested into countless forms, the concept of the limited-self falling away, and recognizing that everything is love… but it happens.

Shifting our perspectives into seeing all as one, happens over a period of time so it can be integrated more easily. The more you adapt to the perspective, the more natural it feels. At some point, the new perspective is not a big deal and becomes the new normal. Seeing yourself in everyone and everything and seeing reality as both the projected reality as well as the physical manifestation of one energy becomes second nature.

However, one of the traps in this process is getting in your 'own way.' For me personally, the concept of ego hasn't always made a ton of sense. The term is thrown around so much that it loses a singular meaning. I have found the word *ego* largely unhelpful. It is one of those words people act like they understand but really don't. The ego is an attachment to the story of who you are and how you perceive the world through your own limited perspective.

Focusing on something much greater than ourselves helps to keep the limited 'self' out of the way. Another way of summarizing this is that you need to get the smaller 'self' out of the way, in order to connect to a larger 'self.' This larger self is the unity of energy with all that is. Some call this "God," some call it Source, and some call it a field of energy. For me, I feel the word, *God*, like some of the other words here, is a bit loaded, and can be confusing and cause issues. I have found that taking the perspective that everything is an infinite field of unconditionally loving energy, has been the most helpful for me.

What do you think or feel when you consider a larger self, or that which is greater than you?

CHAPTER 4

GOING HIGHER: STAGES 1 AND 2

Four Stages

I would like to describe four stages I have found to be essential for shifting to a perspective of the world where you can see 'yourself' in everyone and everything…where you shift to a larger perspective of unity and there is no sense of isolation or being alone. The first two of the four, the victim stage and the giving stage, are discussed below. The next two are discussed in the following chapter.

The Victim Stage

The first of these I labeled the victim stage. In this stage, everything that occurs in your life seems to come from the outside and is happening to you. You are a victim of your circumstances, other people, the environment—well, everything. You are basically an innocent bystander having a lot of terrible things come your way, one after another. I am exaggerating this a bit but will explore more further in the book.

The victim stage is a common stage to be stuck in, and in fact, tends to be the stage where most of humanity seems to feel trapped. It is a place of powerlessness and limitation. Essentially the victim stage involves the belief that when something happens in your life that you do not prefer, it is happening "to you." You believe you have little or no control or power; things happen to you in your life, and you are the victim of whatever happens. In this viewpoint, it is hard to let things go and you are stuck in a perspective of being hurt by others. You do not feel in power to decide, choose, and determine what happens to you.

Giving Stage

The next stage is the giving stage. In this stage, you wake up or are forced to wake up a bit, to see there are other people besides you in the world. It is not just you. More than this, you begin to feel and see there are other people suffering, not just you. I don't mean that you momentarily notice. I mean you *feel* it and it impacts who you actually are. You realize there are others in the world and you must do something, even something small, to help.

In this stage, there is a shift towards seeing what others may want or what may be helpful for them. Moreover, you are shifting your perception to see that by giving to others, *you* also benefit in some way and that we are all interconnected in a larger system. The more positive energy you put out into the world, the more it positively impacts everything, either immediately or over the longer term.

If you can't get past the pain in yourself, you can get stuck in it. The giving stage is an important way to switch to another perspective and to move forward past yourself. Another way of saying this (for example) is the more you focus on the tooth that hurts, the more it will become a distraction and get in the way of bigger things you could focus on. Focusing on something besides yourself when you are suffering can be difficult at first, but then can become easier. It's like a habit where you are trapped in focusing on the pain or addicted to your story. By shifting the focus to something outside of yourself, you begin to shift the pain. Giving to others is in fact (in the larger sense) giving to yourself. In this stage or perspective of giving, you take the pain you have experienced and turn it into fuel for something positive or good.

By giving and focusing on something besides yourself, you are in fact really helping yourself because we are all interconnected as one expansive, energy field manifested in physical form. What you put out is what will eventually come back to you. More than this, we are all energetically intertwined and ultimately all from and a part of the same field of energy and source. Therefore, in this stage, you begin to understand that the fastest way to help yourself heal from pain is to help others.

However, this may take many different forms depending on what is happening to you. For example, if you experienced sexual violence as a child and the abuse impacts you as an adult, it may be too difficult or triggering to help children or adults who are suffering because of child sexual abuse. However, if you are healed to a certain extent, it could be helpful to help children or adults who experienced something similar to you. Healing largely depends on what you feel best connects with you and what you are drawn to. Use your intuition to see what you are drawn to and what speaks to your soul and heart. Each person can take numerous healing paths. However, the most powerful ones are the ones that you yourself are drawn to. If your soul feels connected to teaching music, do that. If it feels drawn to tutoring at-risk, vulnerable children, do that. If there is anything that lights you up and makes you feel alive and joyful while giving, that is the direction to go. If you don't know or can't figure out what lights you up, just try some new things. Feel them out! The best way is to go out there, see what works for you, and see what you connect with.

When it comes to giving, you can be surprised by what lights you up. The most important thing is that you try something, and don't give up on it. If you try working at a soup kitchen or with the homeless and do not feel connected to it or feel repelled by it, that's okay. Don't give up on it. Something else may be better suited for your healing and may help shift you away from the focus on the self. Keep trying. I believe every soul knows exactly how it needs to heal and what it needs to do in order to heal from the victim stage. The way to heal from the victim stage is to step into the giving stage. Whether you are ready or not, just start. Take baby steps, even if it's just helping out a friend unexpectedly or spending a little extra time playing with your pet. It doesn't matter. Just start today, now, right now in this instant.

Because we are so interconnected, when we focus on helping to increase the happiness of others, we are indirectly also increasing the happiness of ourselves and helping ourselves. This is not a one-to-one formula in the sense that you can expect it to work immediately. It is, however, a step toward a life with less suffering and faster, easier transmutation and understanding of pain. It also gives you tools to get unstuck in an otherwise seemingly endless cycle of pain. Therefore, start giving now. Find small ways or just new things to start, but start today, and do something intentionally nice for someone every day. This is a huge part of getting out of the cycle of the victim stage. By the way, you are a person too and so giving to yourself also has a strong impact in the giving stage. The point is just to give something positive instead of negative to the world.

CHAPTER 5

GOING HIGHER: STAGES 3 AND 4

The Shifting Stage

The third stage I propose is the shifting stage. In this stage, the concept of the self shifts more. The more you give to others in the giving stage, the less there seems to be a "me" and "you," and the more you can feel the interconnection between yourself and others. During the transition between the giving and shifting stages, you may start to see yourself in others. You begin to feel less that there is a "you" and "others," and more that others are part of you and you are part of them. Giving to another becomes the same as giving to yourself. During the transition into the shifting stage, your sense of self shifts. You start to see that you are not just "*you.*" You are the whole freaking everything! You expand your vision to see that you are part of a larger stream of energy and all that exists. You are an energetic being and exist in something so much greater than you may have realized.

In this stage, your view of reality is shifting and you are starting to see how everything is actually here to help you evolve and grow to your highest purpose and highest level of self. There begins to be a shift from 1) wondering why is this happening to you... to 2) determining how to transform an experience so it's not hurting you and 3) realizing there is more going on in reality than just your individual perspective. There are larger forces organizing and supporting your life for some bigger purpose. These larger forces push you towards greater levels of personal development, growth, and insight into the nature of reality through every event you experience.

It is called the shifting stage because your concept of self, shifts. In the first stage, you see everything as happening to you and are very self-focused. Your concept of things outside of you is how they benefit you, are neutral to you, or hurt you. In essence, the world mostly revolves around you and the things that are happening to you. This may sound narcissistic but it isn't entirely; it's more about a fear of survival and fear of the self being okay. In the second stage, the giving stage, you wake up to see that the world is not just about you and the things happening to you. In the giving stage, you see the world is also about others, and that others suffer as you do. Essentially, you see that we are all in this together. There is no one who does not have to navigate the human condition and experience pain from being human. In the third stage, the shifting stage, you go beyond seeing yourself and others. In Buddhism, this is referred to as stream entering, where you see and experience that life is a flow, a collective stream of consciousness and energy. In the third stage, you see that there is more than you or others; there is all of reality and life and it is all one energy that flows.

In the shifting stage, there is no real separation between you and others. When you have the experience of truly getting yourself out of the way, you are opened up to the grand reality of the vastness of being. You have the realization that everything is in fact energy and you are a manifestation of this energy. Beyond this, what you think of as yourself has more than just the outer physical projection of yourself. What you are, in another possibly more important way, is an energy body. Your repeating (conscious and unconscious) thoughts, feelings, and emotions create a cycle of patterns. It's like a reoccurring loop that repeats itself and appears to form a personality or self. Similar to a software program downloaded onto a computer, the self is in fact a pattern of behaviors, perspectives, thoughts, feelings, and beliefs. This does not mean the self is not real. The self is very important for functioning in the world. However, there is more to you than just the small self and a life lived only knowing the small self and the perspective of the small self is not a full life. There is so much more beyond this.

When going through the shifting stage, you learn that there is so much more than just your own perspective. There is a connection and unity with all of reality. When you get out of the way, your eyes are opened to an amazing number of things you never saw or experienced before. You start to see that you are part of the expression of everything that exists and could exist. With this vision and insight, there is also a shift into seeing that everything is energy in expression. Specifically, it is comprised of the energy of love and everything is a field of love in manifested form. Like layers of vision or lenses, at the different layers, you begin to understand that everything is in fact, love. On the most obvious outer level, everything appears to be physical and solid. However, there are more layers than this.

When you are in the shifting stage, you are shifting from 1) seeing life as only about "me" to 2) doing things for "others" to 3) a deeper level of reality that has always been there but was somehow unable to be experienced before. It's like cracking through a shell where you see reality as 1) me, 2) others, or the physical, then 3) something beyond all of that but within that.

The reason there is so much focus from many spiritual teachers on the present moment is largely that it is an entrance point for getting past the attachment to "me" and "others" in physical reality. When individuals focus on the present moment, the patterns, behaviors, thoughts, and feelings of the "self" are dismantled while in that state. In the present moment, the harmful repeating patterns existing in physical reality lose their power and momentum. In a true present-moment state, the identity of the self takes a vacation and it doesn't usually need to be functioning for any real reason. More than this, in the present moment, the experience of separation, isolation, attachment, and judgment slows. It is an opening to experiencing that which is beyond the physical and for getting the self out of the way. Practicing the present moment and living in the present moment is a powerful way to go beyond the normal cycles and traps we often fall into with our thoughts, feelings, and emotions. The present moment is a pattern breaker. It brings notice, attention, and awareness to any situation. In the light of awareness, many harmful patterns and negative things cannot survive.

The Infinity Stage

Beyond the experience of realizing "me" and then "others" and then shifting perspective, there is more. There continues to be more. This includes experiencing all of life as a flow, a stream of energy. The experience of this flow can come sooner, but it has greater significance from different perspectives. Eventually, it shifts so you become the flow itself and openness itself. Becoming the flow itself means there is an energy that flows through you and picks up speed. This is the fourth stage or the infinity stage.

In this stage, you understand deeper levels of manifestation, quantum shifting, and the power that our words, thoughts, writing, and imagination have. Becoming the flow means that time shifts so that every moment feels like infinity and the present moment, and yet things shift very quickly. Synchronicity happens instantly and almost as soon as you think or need something, it often somehow appears. Reality shifts from things happening to you in the victim stage to you becoming a smaller determinant of reality itself within the larger field of reality. It is not exactly like reality is a projection or a movie, as many have discussed, particularly Buddhists. This is one way of seeing it but it is more that reality can be shifted differently than just by force, as has been thought in the past. There is much more than force. Force will become increasingly ineffective in the future as we progress further into understanding energy and the importance of energy and intention as a powerful determinant in the form reality takes.

The openness comes from also being open to whatever other information or insights are yet to come. One of the issues with the stages is they are not necessarily linear. They are more complicated and multifaceted than this. It is possible that someone can experience and have insights regarding the self and others, then shift into seeing and experiencing reality as a field of energy in manifested form as well as a field of love. Even then, someone can still fall back into stage one in certain things and fall back into the self-focused "me" perspective. This is okay. The best perspective to take with this is a nonjudgmental and open perspective. However, the process of becoming a fuller version of you occurs, it is always perfect and okay. Maintaining a sense of openness and humility is important to remain beyond the "me" and "others" stage. Humility is useful because it helps to bypass many of the issues of "me." However, this humility is not self-effacing or judgmental of the self; it is more of an open humility.

In the infinity stage, you begin to experience, understand, see, and know that there is no actual separation between you and others, all of life, and everything you can see and not see. This includes everything that will be, has been, or could be. There are endless opportunities. The reality of life is that it is limitless and comprised of limitless energy; you are a manifestation of that energy. You are open to whatever may come or could come in the future and no longer feel afraid of anything. If fear arises, you merely notice it and see it as an energy to be intentionally transformed. Feeling fear or other emotions should not cause fear.

In this stage, the realizations of the third stage and the flow of life continue and expand outward. The flow and expansion increase further until you see and realize that everything is infinite. Everything is an energetic field of love in both un-manifested and manifested forms. There is a deep stillness within you and within this energy. And from all stillness arises form and movement. Another way of understanding the fourth stage of openness, infinity, and a field of love, is that life is like a canvas with a painting on it. The canvas is the un-manifested form; the painting is what manifests into form. There are many unformed possibilities. In fact, it is arguable there are infinite unformed possibilities.

Living in a state of 'being', is the best way to access the insight and connection to this other dimension of living. Participating in retreats and practicing living in the present moment are wonderful ways to drop into this space. There we can connect with the dimension of ourselves and life that is beyond the physical manifestation of form that we see and the stories we attach to that form.

It is a seeing beyond our normal seeing.

Important Considerations for Stages 3 & 4: Namelessness and Flow

Namelessness

An important part of shifting into the perspectives that encompass the third and fourth stages is namelessness and flow. This refers to a detached, peaceful perspective without attached labeling and categorization. This means living in a way that is open and in connection and rhythm with something greater than yourself and even others.

I remember having some experiences seeing through the veil of projected physical reality as a child. When I was seven or eight years old, one of my favorite activities was lying in our hammock under the oak trees in my childhood home in California. I would just rock back and forth and stare at the leaves of the oak tree, the sky, and the clouds for hours. Sometimes I would rock and sometimes I would just lay there. In those moments, I felt that there was no separation between me and the sky, the leaves, or the clouds. I felt and saw this amazing flow, peace, and harmony. It felt like being supported by some kind of state of bliss. It was perfection. I was lost in the sky, the clouds, the breeze, the smell of nature and trees. Time felt like it stopped and all that I was experiencing was all that existed. "I" was gone and became whatever my consciousness focused on at the time.

When I was seven years old, we moved to a house in a more rural area, and at night the sky would light up with stars. It's not the same as going to the middle of a desert and seeing the stars at night of course, but it was pretty spectacular for me. I also used to love to come out at night, breathe in the cool night air mixed in with a warm breeze during the summer, and stare up at the sky. I felt I was home, like somehow all of time and space stopped and I was completely one with everything I was experiencing and seeing. There seemed to be no separation between me and the stars, or me and the sky. It was like some kind of starry heaven, some sort of special bliss. I never talked about these experiences. Somehow, I felt others wouldn't understand. I was also private about them. I didn't announce to everyone that I was going outside to stare at the stars to feel unity, infinity, love, bliss, and timelessness with all that is. I didn't have words for it either. It just felt natural and personal, and something that called me to connect with it. I knew I was drawn to experiencing this namelessness and to not talk about it with anyone.

Besides, we don't really have words to describe it accurately anyway. This nameless, wordless experience drew me to it as much as possible. I lived and experienced my own private heaven and unity. As I got older, the appearances of the outer world, the worry and pain of family, friends, and the stress of life activities started to creep in more and these moments got lost—but not ever completely.

I still continued to connect with the starry night and the unity of nature. I would also go on long runs in high school. I would take random, I suppose you could call them intuitive, pauses, and just stare at a tree, or stare at the sky and hills. I felt unity, infinity, and timelessness and I was lost in these things. I was these things and they were me. Sometimes I would become so absorbed in it, my mom would worry because I would be running when I was sixteen years old for two hours and get back when it was dark. I was running but it was more of a spiritual practice for me. I would stop and stare at trees and the view of hills and nature around me for thirty minutes or more. I wanted to experience that unity and connection. I didn't really have words to express any of this or share it with anyone. To be honest, this is the first time I'm putting it all down on paper for someone to read. This was something I intuitively did and was drawn to doing regularly. No one taught me. It was a knowing and connection that I kept with me every day, no matter what was going on in my outer life.

It was like food for me. I needed it and felt it called to me to connect with it daily. That connection and source are always with you; you just need to see it.

Flow

Following through with purpose is the fastest way to connect deeply with the stream, with the flow, and to connect with greater insights about yourself.

I have realized and come to terms with recently is that just because a person has a destiny or feels he or she has a mission to accomplish something doesn't mean the person will do it. You may or may not in fact accomplish your mission or your purpose. You have to follow through with it and take appropriate action. Larger forces may support you, but in the end, you are the one who must close your eyes, step forward bravely, and act. You must actively create the space and commitment to fulfill your purpose in order to connect and understand it.

One way to simply start is to drop into yourself or your soul every day. Sit quietly with yourself every day until you feel you are dropping into a deeper place of connectedness and can feel what your 'self' is asking for. Write, journal, speak, or express yourself however you can, and whatever comes to you while paying attention to yourself and acting from this place of being. The deeper you drop into yourself and the stillness that exists within, the easier it is to see the layers and projections of the outer world fall away so that the world becomes one field of the energy of love manifested in form.

If this is confusing at all, that is totally okay. The important thing is that this is all experiential. The words here are just pointers to the experience. This is something that must be practiced, allowed in, and experienced. When you have experiences of flow, being in a stream of life, and connected to that which is greater than you, don't cling to it. Like a butterfly, it must be okay for it to come and go. Cling to nothing, not even a field of love. This is part of the ongoing experience of integrating further and deeper into the experience that everything is one field of energy. Knowing that it is an integration process helps with allowing the ebbs and flows and the rising and falling tides of experience. No experience is forever; everything is temporary. The only thing that lasts is the existence of this limitless energy field that we may get glimpses into.

The deeper you drop within, and drop into the stillness, the deeper you connect with un-manifested aspects of reality. The world is comprised of the manifested and un-manifested. The manifested, or the outer projection of reality which appears solid and unchanging, comes from the un-manifested energy that comes forward into the world. To put it simply, everything is energy. The energy that has formed itself into solid-appearing reality is the manifested energy, or energy that comes into form. The energy that we can't see yet and has not come into form is "unmanifested." If this is confusing at all, that's okay. It will come in time.

Take *the perspective and belief* that all of this isn't a big deal at all and you always and easily understand and connect with it. If you hold a *belief* that this is confusing, you can't understand it or won't ever understand it, it just reinforces the experience. This negative belief keeps it farther from you and the universe conforms to this belief. Our conscious and unconscious beliefs largely form our realities and the ongoing experience of our realities.

Imagine every belief you have is a wish. What are you really wishing for?

Take it lightly, and choose your beliefs wisely.

Infinity Stage: Everything is Energy in Manifested Form

As humans, we are very special. Every moment of our lives is best lived by being present and in the now. We are missing our lives if we are not fully living them in the present. However, our lives are much more than what we can see with our eyes, hear with our ears, or sense with our bodies. For example, reflect on an ant or a fish. An ant can only see and hear what an ant can see and hear, and a fish can only understand and see what it can see. A dog is more developed than either, but it also is limited in its perception and understanding of reality. Like the ant, the dog, or the fish, we can only experience what we can experience with our human senses. However, unlike the dog, fish, or ant, we can question our own reality and have insights into the nature of reality and why life is the way it is. We can have a level of introspection that no other creature on earth can. We are special—extremely special.

Please realize I am not saying we are special, meaning we are superior or should abuse or dominate other creatures. If anything, being special means we have a special responsibility to the earth and everything on the earth. In fact, many animals are more in the flow and in tune with larger universal forces than we are. We can say it is instinct, but it can be more than that. Look at the ways that fish swim in schools, or birds fly in flocks. These things happen naturally and in flow with the rhythm of nature. However, we are special because we can reflect on the nature of the self, the nature of reality, and the meaning of others in our lives. We can reach the deepest realizations and inner understandings of any creature on earth.

Infinity Stage: Shifting Up

The big breakthrough I had was that the earth is not how we have been taught it is in school. Wait, what? What the hell is this girl saying? Well, I will walk you through it. First, please keep in mind that for a very long time, people thought that the earth was flat and if you sailed far enough on the water you would fall off. Then it was a big deal when people said the earth was round. This was blasphemy! It upset a lot of people. My own insight takes this some steps further. The earth is round from the perspective of what our human eyes and brains can measure and understand. However, there is so much more than this. There is the collective world energy. There is the river beneath the river, or stream beneath the stream. The layer within and behind it is pure love energy. Seeing these layers of reality affects your daily reality and how you feel and see things. It's like being bathed in love energy all the time and seeing the two layers of reality mixed together.

Being in the present moment is a critical component of diving into the field of the limitless love that is already all around you. By being happy and immersed in the present moment, you are in the now and connected to all that is. All of time exists now and is in the current moment. It does not exist outside of the present moment. All that is, everything that is in the future and past and across all time, dimension, space, and reality exists now and can be connected to and with now. The best way to practice being in the present moment is to practice mindfulness and train your mind to become aware of each and every moment that passes. This means watching each moment and understanding that reality is more like a cartoon with individual pictures (i.e., moments) being flipped through than it is a linear time. Reality is comprised of countless moments. The more aware we are of the moments, the more that time can seem to expand and the deeper the experience that each moment can seem.

In "Auguries of Innocence," poet William Blake writes of a similar experience: "To see a World in a Grain of Sand / And a Heaven in a Wild Flower / Hold Infinity in the palm of your hand / And Eternity in an hour."[1] This is exactly the experience that can happen by looking at and shifting your observation of a table, for example. You can take any object; it doesn't matter. It can help if it is something that is more emotionally neutral. For example, if you are focusing on your favorite food, you may have many emotions, thoughts, feelings, or attachments to that food. If you focus on something you don't like or have an issue with, that can also evoke many emotions, thoughts, and feelings, and often resistance to those things. When starting out, I recommend writing daily affirmations and journaling things like the following.

---

1   William Blake, "Auguries of Innocence," Poetry Foundation, accessed February 14, 2023, https://www.poetryfoundation.org/poems/43650/auguries-of-innocence.

"Of course, I see reality, and all layers, lenses, and aspects of true reality."

"Of course, I always see everything completely and absolutely clearly."

"I love and am so excited by how clearly I see everything, and the layers of reality I can so amazingly and clearly see."

"I can't believe how amazingly beautiful reality truly is!"

"Reality is gorgeous, incredible, and full of love and wonder!"

Try different affirmations or journaling to discover which resonates most with you. The more you experience these affirmations, and practice writing them regularly, the more affirmations will flow from and come to you. First, state the intention of what you want to experience and see, and make sure it connects and resonates with you. Next, I recommend choosing something neutral to begin observing and connecting with. Examples include a table, a chair, or a jacket. It is helpful if you feel neutral about the object, which means there aren't a lot of feelings, images, or reactions about it. You can just look at it and observe it as it is. This means you are looking at the projection, at the image you are seeing of a table, a chair, a jacket, or whatever you chose to observe. A meditation practice where you keep your eyes open but resting still on an object can be effective for this.

You may need to look at this object for five minutes a day, for one hour a day, or maybe for eight hours straight. I once did a thirty-day silent meditation retreat where we were instructed to stare, just stare, at a tree while sitting in a chair for three days straight. We took breaks for eating, sleeping, and going to the bathroom. Otherwise, we sat for three days, stared at the trees, and concentrated on one particular tree. As time passed, we began to see it as a projected image of a tree. In fact, that is the breakthrough: *everything* is a projected image. Throughout and within the projected image is energy—beautiful, pure energy. Beautiful, pure light is interwoven throughout and within everything. Within this beautiful, pure energy that comprises and makes up all that exists, will exist, and has existed, is an overflowing beautiful energy of love—pure love. This is the feeling and experience of pure, limitless, amazing love.

You can increase your level of practice and further integrate foundational principles by practicing this love perspective on yourself, with romantic relationships, friendships, work situations, and things that cause pain.

CHAPTER 6

OPENING UP

Infinity Stage: Living in a State of Love-Centered Being

Living in a state of love-centered being means that you experience a state and flow of love no matter what is happening in the outer projection of life. You are no longer practicing "on something;" you are in fact becoming the existence of love and the embodiment of love. From this state, you don't need to practice with anything at all; you just are it. You decide to be it. Cultivate a continuous state of love and being in the present moment as part of your ongoing daily lived experience. Daily journaling to cultivate this present moment love-centered being can be effective despite whatever is happening in your life. Below are some effective affirmations and mantras to practice regularly.

Of course, I am full of love and happiness.
Of course, I feel completely in the present moment every moment of every day.
Of course, I am totally in the now at all times of the day.
I am so happy I am full of peace, feelings of ease, and contentment.
Of course, I am so incredibly successful at everything I do or try.
Of course, I am surrounded by a limitless field of love that I feel bathed in every day.

Daily affirmations to cultivate this present moment love-centered being

I am the embodiment of love.
I see and experience a field of love in everything and everywhere.
I am always fully supported and feel fully supported.
I am always feeling centered and at peace.
I am always living in the present moment.
I am always in the now.

Meditations and daily activities can cultivate more of a love-centered approach. Some activities can include watching sunsets and trees, observing bodies of water, being around the ocean, being in nature, and practicing being and feeling love at the same time. The key is to be. It is about "being" the thing, not doing the thing. Focusing on an emotion of being increases the experience of love-centeredness.

Love-centered being incorporates the elements of being in the present moment and the energy of love together. Much of what is taught about mindfulness and being in the present moment omits or barely talks about love. However, when you truly exist in the present moment and live from a moment-to-moment experience, love and the overwhelming nature of love in the fabric of reality pours over you. Love is a critical, interwoven component of the present moment and being in the present.

Being in the present moment naturally brings out this understanding and exposes deeper levels of the energy of love all around you and in everything you see. You can begin to see that the energy of love is all there is in reality, and it bathes, covers, and supports you and everything in all ways. The energy of love is the is-ness of everything and is always there when you have eyes to see. The energy of love centers you, gives focus and clarity, soothes you, is always with you, and brings you into the present moment. The energy of love gives a hopeful light feeling of the future where the things that made you feel stuck or weighed down no longer matter in the same way, if they matter much at all.

Life is in many ways about perspective and the lens through which we view our world. Enlightenment or insights on the path of enlightenment as I understand it, are merely ongoing changes in perspective and seeing life from a different, clearer lens. It is possible that the difference between being stuck in ego and self-centeredness versus shifting into a perspective of enlightenment is merely a new lens from which to view the world. For example, one moment you are focused on yourself and see life as happening to you. You are the focus of the world and everything that is happening is happening outside of you and directed at you. A shift in perspective can occur when you take the pain that you experienced from outside influences and turn it into something positive.

There is an expression that says, "No mud, no lotus." This is frequently used in mindfulness and meditation situations to help practitioners understand that what happens to them in their lives, and any trauma, pain, or hurt, can be transformed into something beautiful. Although our pain and hurt can feel almost stuck to us, or stuck in our energy and taken on a life of its own, this pain can make us unintentionally stuck. We can become trapped in focusing on ourselves without meaning to do so. Our pain from past things that have happened to us can get in the way and we can become unintentionally self-centered. It is not intentional, of course. The more pain we are in, the more it becomes all we can think about. For example, imagine if you have severe pain in your tooth. It can be hard to think about other things besides this. It can become all-consuming. You may find yourself unintentionally complaining frequently of the pain in your tooth, how it's affecting your day, and is giving you a headache. You can't eat, talk very much, concentrate, or sleep because it is so extremely uncomfortable. Your tooth can become the center of your focus, the most important thing while it's hurting. All you might be able to think of is your tooth and how you are feeling. This is similar in a way to what can happen in the victim stage. In the victim stage, you can become consumed by the pain you are feeling and what has happened to you. Because of the discomfort and immense pain, you may be experiencing from this perspective, it can be difficult to get out of it.

Mantra

May you flow in the stream with ease, grace, and security, feeling it all around you, supporting you, carrying you through all moments in life. You feel like you are being supported by a cloud that is carrying you.
This stream is love
The essence of love

Guided Meditation

Breathe in and out, releasing all fears, all blocks
Clear all and any blocks in and throughout your energy
Continue shifting and clearing,
Shifting and clearing,
Letting go and clearing out all blocks
Across all time, dimension, space, and reality

Imagine that you bring your energy up 100 feet and expand it out 100 feet wide
Feel lighter and lighter, lighter and lighter
See yourself go higher and higher, lighter and lighter
Expand and lift your energy higher, imagine 300 feet higher, 500 feet higher, 1,000 feet, 2,000 feet

3,000 feet
10,000 feet
Imagine your energy expanding out 300 feet, 500 feet, 1,000
feet, 2,000 feet, 3,000 feet, and 10,000 feet

Now see an abundance of light pouring down across all of
your energy,
Clearing all blocks across all time, dimension, space, and reality
Imagine your energy expanding out to encompass all that is,
will be, and could be across the entire universe, past, present
and future
Imagine beautiful light of whatever color(s) most resonate
with you pouring through and washing away all blocks and
anything heavy

Expand your energy out farther and farther, lighter and lighter
You are now released and free from all heaviness and weight
holding you down in any way
You feel lighter than you've ever felt before
Any heaviness has left
You are floating in a stream of love—no blocks, no weight
Your life has become a stream,
A clearer understanding of reality covers you
You are immersed in the energy of pure love,
Feeling completely safe, secure, and centered

Guided Energy Shift

Take a deep breath in, hold it, and then let a deep breath out
Take another deep breath in, hold it, and then exhale deeply
Take one last slow, deep breath in, then slowly breathe out
Count down 5, 4, 3, 2, 1
You are in a deep rest, with a sense of peace and letting go

In this calmer state, imagine there is a beautiful bonfire of
incredibly bright flames
This bonfire burns up anything and everything that is no
longer helping you and all blocks in the way of your life
becoming better
Hold a piece of paper, with everything that is blocking you,
making you unhappy, or getting in the way of you becoming
the fullest truest version of yourself written on it
Put this piece of paper into the bonfire. The paper burns away,
the smoke and ashes are carried away, and you are free of those
blocks. Your life is becoming better every day in every way.

Walking away from the bonfire with all those changes having
happened, you see you are holding three white balloons. These
are wish balloons and allow for any wish you have to come
true. Look at each balloon and imagine what your wish is.
Breathe in your wish and breathe out your wish, letting the
balloon go.

*Know that your life is getting better every day in every way,
and you are always feeling lighter and lighter, lighter and lighter*

*Then imagine there is a beautiful light above your head, going
through the top of your head, and going from above to below,
below to above, filling up every atom, molecule, or particle.
Go into this light and float past the earth, moon, planets, and
stars, all the way out to an area of pure darkness and pure
white potential. Go through a door. Closing it, you encounter
another version of yourself. This version is filled with joy and
peace, and is the version of yourself that feels fully true, fully
you. It is the you that feels most aligned and in the state of
flow and bliss.*

Count 3, 2, 1 and shift to this version of yourself now.

*You are now this version of yourself. Feel full, unconditional
love and acceptance of yourself, and know that your life is
always getting better and better every day, in every way.*

*Open your eyes, counting 1, 2, 3, and slowly come back to
this present moment, experiencing this new version of who
you are.*

Infinity Stage: Shift into the Amazing Feeling You!

Love-centered living from the fourth stage is also about how you feel and being in a state of radical acceptance no matter what the outer circumstances may be. Fierce love means that you can withstand anything because the ground you stand on is groundless. It is a stream of love that surrounds you and goes beyond the outer projection of reality. It allows you to stay calm and centered in even the most difficult of storms and situations. Love-centered living helps you shift into an understanding that everything can be here to help you when you gain perspective and also to help you gain compassion and empathy for what others may be going through. This allows forgiveness and self-compassion and a letting go of things that have hurt you.

Letting things go and seeing how they could have helped or transformed your life or how they can still transform your life can be a source of healing. It is fairly normal for individuals to hold onto things and hold onto their old, heavy selves when they feel they've been hurt. It's often hard to let go when we can't understand why something happened and the benefits of it. Seeing from the perspective that everything is happening to help us grow and that everything is helping us, can shift and change things. This does not mean blinding ourselves to the truth of situations and circumstances or lying to ourselves with ridiculous reframing that is just a cover-up for how we really feel. Letting go is meant to help us see reality more clearly and from a larger perspective.

We live in a seemingly dualistic world, where we see certain things as good and bad and label everything. We like to label things as good, bad, or neutral. However, that which causes pain now may lead to something positive later, and that which seems positive now may lead to pain later. For this reason, it is important not to cling or be too attached to anything. Reality is constantly shifting and everything is here to help us reach deeper levels of realization. This work is never done; there are always deeper levels to go. It is impossible for anything good, bad, or neutral to not make an impact on our lives for this ultimate goal.

Allow the things in your life to transform you into an unstoppable, lightest you. Anything—absolutely anything—can do this. Transformation can come from looking at a beautiful sunset, opening your heart and soul, and connecting with the oneness and realization that all is one. It can come from sitting in a hospital with someone you love more than life itself who has been hospitalized for three weeks. It can come from working with human trafficking survivors but seeing 'yourself' in them, in another form.

You are able to turn anything—absolutely anything—into a deeper level of realization and insight. The deeper these levels of insight and realization, the easier life becomes no matter what happens. It doesn't mean you stop having hard times. In fact, you may even start to have more, but this only strengthens, deepens, and increases your level of growth. In addition, you are able to move through challenges and understand them better. It's almost like life's way of saying, "You think you learned this? Let's try it from this angle and see how you feel, or this angle. Let's see how well you've mastered this insight, this perspective, and what you've learned."

Like a mindful ninja, you can move the way that life moves, flow the way life flows. You can dance each day with life, with God. You can always feel totally supported by the universe in knowing that whatever happens, your mindful perspective, love, connection, and insight carry you through everything.

Take advantage of everything this life has to offer: all the realizations, insights, and discoveries of everything that come from living on this beautiful Earth. You can connect to and access what you are looking for with love and connection now. Fully and completely embrace this world, this moment, and this life, and decide to receive all that it has to give. You won't be disappointed by the extraordinary connection, love, expansion, and insight you receive.

With so, so much love always and forever, ☺

BIBLIOGRAPHY

Blake, William. "Auguries of Innocence."
Poetry Foundation. Accessed February 14, 2023.
https://www.poetryfoundation.org/poems/43650/
auguries-of-innocence.

AUTHOR'S NOTE:

I would love to work with you further on these things and on gaining deeper levels of understanding in your life. Please check out www.drsaraspowart.com or www.happinesslearned.com to contact me or to work with me personally. I provide both in-person and remote counseling and coaching services. I can also be seen on my "Happiness Learned" Facebook and Instagram pages and YouTube. In addition to this, I have created a six-week happiness training course that you can contact me about at www.drsaraspowart.com. or through my LLC, Happiness Learned.